D0805660

I Must Go Down to the Beach Again

to the

Beach Again

and Other Poems

Karen Jo Shapiro

ILLUSTRATED BY Judy Love

I Must Go Down to the Beach Again

and Other Poems

ini Charlesbridge

Contents

Read poems along with me—
The rest is yet to be.

(With apologies to Robert Browning)

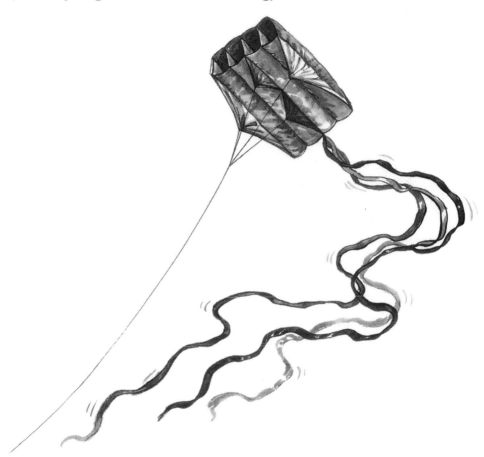

Author's Note:

The poems that follow are parodies: bits of silliness, humor, or everyday life inspired by some of the classic poems in English and American literature. Imitation is sometimes called the sincerest form of flattery—and though parodies are often written to make fun of something, these poems spring from deep respect. (And maybe just a little silliness.)

My Letter from the World

With apologies to Emily Dickinson
("This Is My Letter to the World")

This is my letter from the world
That once it wrote to me:
"Dear Friend," it spelled, in purple buds
Upon a lilac tree.

"Come look around," the letter said
On mountains topped by snow.
"For if you search a hundred years
There'd still be more to know.

"Please play with me," it wrote in waves
Beneath a bright blue sky,
Then signed itself, "Sincerely, World,"
Upon a butterfly.

About My Baby Sister

With apologies to George Gordon, Lord Byron
("She Walks in Beauty")

She wakes up crying in the night,
Which keeps us all up very late.
She screams for milk with all her might,
Then spits up everything she ate.
Her diapers are a messy sight—
So why does Mom insist she's great?

To My Brother

With apologies to Ben Jonson ("Song, to Celia")

Blink at me only with your eyes,
And I will blink with mine.
Kick at me only with your feet,
And I will start to whine.
Pull at my hair, and I will SCREAM
For Mom and Daddy, too!
But blink at me only with your eyes,
And I'll just blink at you.

My Mouth Closed Twice

With apologies to Emily Dickinson
("My Life Closed Twice Before Its Close")

My mouth closed twice before it shut.
It yet remains to hear
If grown-ups will say, "QUIET DOWN!"
Again into my ear.

I've tried to quiet down three times,
But words keep bursting out.
I have so much I want to say—
Why won't they let me shout?

David's Flute

With apologies to William Shakespeare (Henry VIII, *Act III, scene i*)

David, with his plastic flute,
Stomps around and makes it toot,
Then he'll wave it high and low,
Singing EE-I-EE-I-O!

Everyone who hears him play
Laughs and cheers him on his way.
Music sweet and noise so loud,
Made for his adoring crowd.

David with his wooden spoon,
Bangs a pot to make a tune—
Soon it's off to bed he'll go,
Singing EE-I-EE-I-O!

Pass the Pancakes

With apologies to Robert Browning ("Song, from Pippa Passes")

Blueberry batter
Is plopped in a pan.
Dad, in the kitchen,
Cooks fast as he can.
Plates on the table.
Juice on the way.
Dad's home for breakfast—
All's right with the day!

The Sick Tummy

With apologies to William Blake ("The Sick Rose")

Oh, Tummy—you are sick!
I ate a bit too much
Of ice cream on a stick,
And candy bars and such—

Oh, Tummy, I had pie,
Banana bread and cake.
They tasted great—oh, my!
But, Tummy—what an ache!

Soccer Land

With apologies to William Shakespeare
(A Midsummer Night's Dream, *Act II, scene i)*

Over field, over ground,
Through the dirt, through the grass—
Watch me running all around,
Now I dribble, kick, and pass.
I am racing everywhere,
Faster than the ball gets there!
I am on the purple team.
"Go!" I hear the people scream.
Past a bench, then to the post,
Here's the part I like the most:
There is just one minute more—
So I aim, I kick, I SCORE!

July Joy

With apologies to Sara Teasdale ("Joy")

I'm wild today! I could swing from the trees,
To see the parade march by.
I jump and I shout and I let my joy out—
Because it's the Fourth of July.

I've eaten some melon and corn on the cob
With a big piece of warm apple pie.
And oh, what a treat when there's shortcake to eat
On the wonderful Fourth of July.

Now I'm dressed in a hat that is red, white, and blue,
Watching colors spark up in the sky.
There's a bang and a boom, then I see a flash zoom—
Hooray for the Fourth of July!

I Must Go Down to the Beach Again

With apologies to John Masefield ("Sea-Fever")

I must go down to the beach again, where there's water,
  sand, and sky,
And all I ask is my red toy boat with a string to pull it by . . .
And my bathtub duck, and a yellow truck, and my plastic
  squirt-toy spraying—
I'll take them all to the beach with me where I'll spend the
  whole day playing.

I must go down to the beach again, where the games and
  fun begin,
And the water's cold, but I do not mind, so I always jump
  right in.
And all I ask is my blow-up raft to float beneath the sky—
A pail and shovel, towel and hat, and a kite that I can fly.

I must go down to the beach again; there's not much else
   I'll use—
Just these cool green glasses for the sun and a pair of
   water shoes,
A sandwich, plum, and lemonade, some pudding, and
   a spoon,
Yes, I must go down to the beach again! And I'll be
   ready soon. . . .

Never Try to Smell a Bee

With apologies to William Blake ("Love's Secret")

Never try to smell a bee
Or put peach jelly on your knee,
And if a bear sleeps near a tree,
Make sure you walk by carefully.

I sniffed a bee! I sniffed a bee!
He stung me on my jelly knee!
I yelled so loud beside the tree,
The bear woke up and charged at me!

He was so big, I had to flee.
I ran away with my stung knee.
The story, though, ends happily:
The bear was not as fast as me!

The Smells

With apologies to Edgar Allan Poe ("The Bells")

I.

Use your nose and find the smells!
All the smells!
What a lot of different things your sniffing nose foretells!
Springtime smells are sure to please—
The scent of lilacs on the breeze,
Roses, tulips, just-mowed grass—
Lots of pretty smells will pass.

But what about the yucky smells?
The now-you're-not-so-lucky smells!
When spring cleaning, there's no doubt:
Some smells you're better off without.
Like rotten eggs and cheese that's old,
Mothballs, mildew, must, and mold.
In the basement there's the stench
Of dirty laundry on a bench,
In the yard there's doggy-doo,
And if you get some on your shoe,
You will want to shout *pee-yew*!
Oh, the smells, smells, smells, smells,
Smells, smells, smells!

II.

School is out, so find the smells.
Summer smells!
Salty seashore, sunscreen, shells,
Burgers cooking on a grill,
Evening air that's sweet and still—

But what about repulsive smells?
The awful, horrid, you-might-get-convulsive smells!
Garbage dumpsters in the heat—
Rotting fish and spoiled meat.
Outhouses are stinky, too,
So if there's business you must do
I think that you will cry *pee-yew*!
Oh, the smells, smells, smells, smells,
Smells, smells, smells!

III.

Ready, set, and find the smells—
Autumn smells!
Pine trees, air that's crisp and cool,
Sharpened pencils new for school,
Applesauce and pumpkin pie—
Lots of yummy scents go by.

But what about the rotten smells?
The wish-they-were-forgotten smells!
Like the stomach-turning stink
Of sour milk you try to drink
Or filthy sponges in the sink;
Mildewed leaves so rank and vile,
Horse manure in a pile.
If you sniff while passing through
You might want to say *pee-yew*!
Oh, the smells, smells, smells, smells,
Smells, smells, smells!

IV.

Bundle up and find the smells—
Winter smells!
First the fragrance, waking up,
Of steaming cocoa in your cup.
Then later when you've come from play—
MMM! Fresh-baked cookies on a tray.
And when you're outside, let me know
Is there—sniff, sniff—a smell of snow?

But what about the foul smells,
The plug-your-nose-up-with-a-towel smells?
Like bad-news baby bowel smells
Of diaper pails left full indoors
When it's too cold to do the chores.
Or what about a turkey stew that's been around a month
    or two?
If someone serves this meal to you—
I'll bet you want to scream *pee-yew*!
Oh, the smells, smells, smells, smells,
Smells, smells, smells!

Please turn your nose away, my dear.
You've had enough smells for the year.

This Rotten, Lousy Flu

With apologies to George Gordon, Lord Byron
("So We'll Go No More A-Roving")

So, our noses we'll be blowing
And we'll cough until we wheeze—
Oh, outside it might be snowing,
But we sit inside and sneeze.

There is nowhere that we're going
There is nothing we can do—
So, our boredom just keeps growing
With this rotten, lousy flu!

Now our heads are hot and sticky,
But our bodies have a chill.
Oh, our stomachs sure feel icky—
It's just NO fun being ill!

We don't mean to be picky—
But we're feeling kind of blue—
Because even sleeping's tricky
With this rotten, lousy flu!

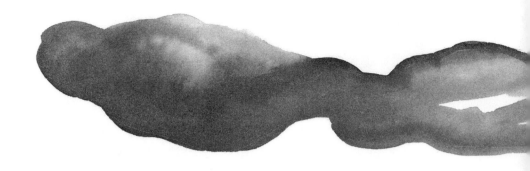

Don't Let the Toast Burn

With apologies to Richard Brinsley Sheridan
("Here's to the Maiden of Bashful Fifteen")

Here's to the white bread that I love so much—
When toasted, it's beautifully browned.
Here's to whole wheat, warm and soft to the touch—
Delicious with jam spread around!

First thing I must learn:
Don't let the toast burn.
I like it the most when I don't burn the toast.

Here's to French toast made with egg-battered bread—
Add syrup and it's sure to please.
Here's to a lunch where I feel nicely fed
By a sandwich of toasted grilled cheese.

It needs a good turn—
Don't let the toast burn!
A wonderful host keeps an eye on the toast.

For let it be thick-sliced or let it be thin,
Wheat or rye—why, we'll care not a feather—
If you have a toaster, I'll pop the bread in,
And we'll both eat our pieces together.

Now it is your turn:
Don't let the toast burn!
So take up your post—keep your eye on that toast!

Up-Hill

With apologies to Christina Rossetti ("Up-Hill")

Does the toad hop up-hill all the way?
Yes, to the very end.
Does the journey take the whole long day?
From morning to night, my friend.

But what will he do to pass the time
If the miles seem too long?
He'll dip into a puddle of slime
And sing a croaking song.

Will he see more creatures at each stop?
A turtle, snake, and frog.
Will there be a resting place at top?
Yes, under a mossy log.

Is it hard to hop on a hill so steep?
Yes, he's a worn-out toad.
And what does he say as he goes to sleep?
"Oh, how I wish I rode."

Norman's Fancy

With apologies to John Masefield ("Captain Stratton's Fancy")

Oh, my sister loves lime Jell-O, and my mom is fond of red—
My daddy won't eat Jell-O; he has cherry pie instead.
But who is it that can't get chocolate mousse out of his head?
Why, I'll tell you—it's my older brother Norman.

Oh, my mommy likes eggs scrambled and my daddy likes
    them fried.
My sister orders omelettes with potatoes on the side.
But an egg made out of chocolate with a caramel goo inside
Is the choice of my older brother Norman.

My mommy loves to drink tea and my dad's the grape
    juice sort.
My sister drinks more milk than I can possibly report.
But do you know who guzzles chocolate syrup by the quart?
Well, of course, it's my older brother Norman.

Yes, now and then my parents have a chocolate bar or two,
My sister likes a piece of chocolate cake some days, it's true—
But who's the one who takes his meals with chocolate
    all day through?
You guessed it: it's my older brother Norman.

My Last Marker

With apologies to Robert Browning ("My Last Duchess")

That's my last marker in the drawer—
I once had seven markers more.
Black is leaking, Red is dried—
Yellow's lost somewhere outside.
Brown spun through the washing machine.
Orange broke. The dog chewed Green.
Purple's wet and works no more.

So, my last marker's in that drawer.
If I had three or even two . . .
But now my world is all in Blue!

The Train Comes, The Train Goes

With apologies to Henry Wadsworth Longfellow
("The Tide Rises, The Tide Falls")

The train comes, the train goes—
The wheels clatter, the whistle blows.
All along the railroad track,
The town folk hear the clickety-clack,
And the train comes, the train goes.

It speeds along, and then it slows;
The engineer waves out hello's.
It pulls into the station stop
With a clippety-clippety clop,
And the train comes, the train goes.

It's half-past nine, the doors close.
Once again the whistle blows.
The people on the platform sigh—
They watch it go and wave good-bye.
For the train comes, the train goes.

One Day I Took a Chance and Wrote a Poem

With apologies to Edmund Spenser
("Amoretti LXXV: One Day I Wrote Her Name Upon the Strand")

One day I took a chance and wrote a poem.
It felt so great to let my words run free.
Now I write outside, in school, at home—
And all my work is always signed "By Me."

If

With apologies to Rudyard Kipling ("If")

If you can't wait to pick a book right now
And read it through until the very end
To find out who did what, and why, and how,
Then—lucky you!—you're a READER, my friend!

There Is No Cleanup Like a Bath

With apologies to Emily Dickinson
("There Is No Frigate Like a Book")

There is no cleanup like a bath
To take my dirt away
When I've been on a muddy path
Or making pots of clay.

However filthy I may get,
I always know there's hope
When sitting in the tub all wet
And lathered up with soap.

Bubbles

*With apologies to William Shakespeare (*Macbeth, *Act IV, scene i)*

Bubbles, bubbles,
Singles and doubles.
Soapy bath and fishy pond—
Blow some from a plastic wand—
Here a moment, then they're gone.

Glad Rest

With apologies to Robert Louis Stevenson ("Requiem")

Under a polka-dotted sheet,
I wear thick socks upon my feet.
Gladly I played; now gladly rest,
My blanket snug across my chest.

My teeth are brushed, as you can see,
My pillow just where it should be;
Turn out the light and off I'll doze—
Warm and cozy to my toes.

Notes on Original Poems and Poets

I have always loved to read and write. As an English major in college, I got to read and study some of the great poems and poets in English and American literature.

Many famous poets write about very serious things: lost love, missed opportunities, or death. I like to lighten the tone of these classic works, so most of my parodies are silly ones. Sometimes I try to change the mood of a poem—making a sad one happy, for example. Other times, I'm trying to update a poem by changing the idea or topic to one that's easier to understand.

I like writing parodies because it's fun to put my own twist on a classic poem. Sometimes a catchy rhythm, or meter, gets into my head and I play around with it to see what other words or phrases can fit the pattern. Other times it's the scene or situation that inspires me to write my own version. And sometimes I get the idea for the parody first: I'll be thinking about a funny situation, and then later I'll find a poem that would be just right to "transform."

What follows here is a list of the original poems and poets. In some cases, I've added a brief note about why I picked this particular poem.

Note: The date following each poem title is the date of first publication. In some cases, poems were published after the poet had died.

Emily Dickinson (1830–1886) "This Is My Letter to the World" 1924

George Gordon, Lord Byron (1788–1824) "She Walks in Beauty" 1815
The first line of this poem, "She walks in Beauty like the Night," is one I remembered from college. The words morphed in my mind to, "She wakes up crying in the night"—which made me think about the many ways that a baby changes a household. I am the oldest child of four, so I can understand the narrator's feelings!

Ben Jonson (1572–1637) "Song, to Celia" 1616

Emily Dickinson (1830–1886) "My Life Closed Twice Before Its Close" 1924

William Shakespeare (1564–1616) *Henry VIII* 1612–1613
I love the songs in Shakespeare's plays—they are fun to change around. In the original verses, Orpheus plays his lute to the delight of nature. That made me think of my son David, who at age two delighted his family with his impromptu musical shows.

Robert Browning (1812–1889) "Song, from Pippa Passes" 1895

William Blake (1757–1827) "The Sick Rose" 1794
Blake is one of my favorite poets to imitate; I like his poems' clear and repeatable rhythms. With this poem, I wondered what other "sick" thing the narrator could be addressing—and an overstuffed tummy came to mind.

William Shakespeare (1564–1616) *A Midsummer Night's Dream* 1594
"Over hill, over dale, through brush, through fire." I once played Theseus in this play, and I remembered hearing these lines as I waited for my entrance. Now, re-reading the piece, I imagined my daughter Elina running fast at her soccer games. I tried to capture the excitement and pride in playing hard and scoring a goal.

Sara Teasdale (1884–1933) "Joy" 1915

In elementary school, Mr. Littlefield and Mr. Walsh, two of my teachers who were passionate about poetry, introduced our class to the lovely works of this poet. When I was a kid, I loved the Fourth of July—the noise and sun, food and fireworks. I used Teasdale's "wild" emotion to bring those memories to the page.

John Masefield (1878–1967) "Sea-Fever" 1902

"I MUST go down to the seas again."
I always loved the sound of this line and the way it repeats. Those same poetry-loving teachers taught our class to learn and recite some poems by heart. This is a poem lots of grownups easily recognize and remember. I kept the idea of the original, but added a few twists to appeal to the kid in me, drawing on my memories of fun times at the beach.

William Blake (1757–1827) "Love's Secret" 1863

Edgar Allan Poe (1809–1849) "The Bells" 1849
I find Poe to be one of the most fascinating poets: His best known poems ("The Raven," "Annabel Lee," and, of course, "The Bells") have such interesting rhythm and rhyme patterns. Here Poe's words were unforgettable: "the bells, bells, bells, bells, bells, bells, bells!" I suspected from my experience around my children and their friends that they would appreciate a poem about all kinds of good and awful smells instead.

George Gordon, Lord Byron (1788–1824) "So We'll Go No More A-Roving" 1830

Richard Brinsley Sheridan (1751–1816) "Here's to the Maiden of Bashful Fifteen" 1777

Christina Rossetti (1830–1894) "Up-Hill" 1861

John Masefield (1878–1967) "Captain Stratton's Fancy" 1903

Robert Browning (1812–1889) "My Last Duchess" 1842
This poem is pretty gloomy—those poor duchesses!
I played around with the first line, "That's my last
duchess," to write a parody that would be lighter
in mood. In our house, it's sadly true that a
box of markers quickly gets misplaced,
dried out, and/or accidentally destroyed.

Henry Wadsworth Longfellow (1807–1882) "The Tide Rises,
The Tide Falls" 1880
I like the way this poem sounds (it does sound like a tide!). My
version isn't a humorous one, but more of a variation on the idea
of a sound that gets louder and softer. Our family is a bunch of
train lovers, and the sound of a train is quite comforting to me.

Edmund Spenser (1552–1599) "Amoretti LXXV: One Day I Wrote
Her Name Upon the Strand" 1595
This poem's first line stuck in my mind from college. I tried to
capture the pride I've seen in children when they first become writers.

Rudyard Kipling (1865–1936) "If" 1910

Emily Dickinson (1830–1886) "There Is No Frigate Like a Book" 1894

William Shakespeare (1564–1616) *Macbeth* 1605–1606

Robert Louis Stevenson (1850–1894) "Requiem" 1887
As a child, one of my first books of
poetry, given to me by my parents,
was Stevenson's *A Child's Garden of
Verses*. The original is about dying: I
saw its possibilities as a poem about
sleep instead. The rhythm of the original
poem sounds to me a bit like a lullaby.

To my wonderful son, David—K. J. S.

To my three muses, Amanda, Dorrie, and Jojo, who have cheered
me on (and up) through the years. With gratitude and love—J. L.

Text copyright © 2007 by Karen Jo Shapiro
Illustrations copyright © 2007 by Judy Love

Published by Charlesbridge
85 Main Street
Watertown, MA 02472
(617) 926-0329
www.charlesbridge.com

Library of Congress Cataloging-in-Publication Data
Shapiro, Karen Jo, 1964–
I must go down to the beach again / Karen Jo Shapiro ; illustrated by Judy Love.
p.   cm.
ISBN 978-1-58089-143-1 (reinforced for library use)
ISBN 978-1-58089-144-8 (softcover)
1. Children's poetry, American. 2. Humorous poetry, American.
3. Parodies. I. Love, Judith DuFour, ill. II. Title.
PS3619.H356I2 2006
811'.54—dc22   2006009029

Printed in the United States of America
(hc) 10 9 8 7 6 5 4 3 2 1
(sc) 10 9 8 7 6 5 4 3 2 1

Illustrations done in ink on Arches watercolor paper
Display type and text type set in Violastix and Caxton
Color separations by Chroma Graphics, Singapore
Printed and bound by Lake Book Manufacturing, Inc.
Production supervision by Brian G. Walker
Designed by Diane M. Earley